LAKELAND LIFE
IN THE 1940s AND 1950s

The Photographs of Gwen Bertelsman

EDITED BY MARTIN VARLEY

HALSGROVE

OF *friends* **THE LAKE DISTRICT**

First published in Great Britain in 2003

British Library Cataloguing-in-Publication Data
A CIP record for this title is available from the British Library

ISBN 1 84114 277 8

HALSGROVE

Halsgrove House
Lower Moor Way
Tiverton, Devon EX16 6SS
Tel: 01884 243242
Fax: 01884 243325
email: sales@halsgrove.com
website: www.halsgrove.com

Printed by D'Auria Industrie Grafiche Spa, Italy

Contents

Introduction

Gwen Bertelsman: a lover of the Lake District

Gwen Bertelsman photographed during her time in the Lake District.

Gwen Bertelsman is not a name readily associated with the Lake District. She was not born here, nor did she die here. An enigmatic figure, none of the people still alive whose pictures appear in this book recall her either as a family friend or as a well-known local figure. She is just remembered as a lady with a car and a camera, who came and went in a day; polite and approachable, but shy and seldom comfortable in the presence of strangers. She was not one prone to stopping for a meal or staying for the night.

But it is perhaps because she had the eyes of an outsider that her images show so naturally the life and landscape of the Lake District in the 1940s and 1950s. There is no prejudice in her pictures, no effort to romanticise the rural scene as Lakeland artists had done before and have done since. These are images of everyday life and cover the period of the Second World War, when life in the Lake District was anything but ordinary, when it had an intensity never seen before or since.

She was in her mid twenties when she arrived in the Lake District at the end of the 1930s. In the few photographs we have of her, she is slim and dark-haired, appearing more suited to the catwalk than the fell walk.

War had already loomed large in her life. She was just two-years old at the start of the First World War, when her Berlin-born parents who had emigrated to England, were interned along with other German nationals. It might have been this experience which prompted her family to drop an 'n' from their surname and make themselves more 'English'.

Home life in the post-war years must have been difficult for Gwen. Before the war her father had been a London diamond dealer, like his father before him. Used to being looked after, her parents eventually sold their house to live in hotels. Gwen was an only child, whose parents felt she was too good to mix with other children, so she was educated at home by a governess.

It was perhaps a reaction against this isolation and lack of belonging which prompted her to move to the Lake District and share, albeit from behind the security of a lens, in the tight-knit community life of wartime and post-war Lakeland.

By now she was beginning to break free of her childhood constraints, and it was during this period that she met Frances and Suzie, two influences pivotal to her time in the Lake District.

Frances Lewis was older than she, a socialist and her mentor, who broadened Gwen's attitude and lifestyle beyond the closeted confinement of her childhood. It was she who moved to the Lake District, to Brockstones, a small cottage above White Moss Common, overlooking Rydal Water, and it was she who persuaded Gwen to leave her job in London as a hospital secretary to join her.

Gwen's companion Frances Lewis outside their house 'Brockstones', at White Moss Common above Rydal Water.

Below: 'Suzie' beside Bassenthwaite Lake.

'Suzie' was an Austin 7 motor car. Gwen worked as an administrator at the Ethel Hedley Children's Orthopaedic Hospital at Calgarth, Windermere, and on her days off she and Suzie would tour the Lakes, indulging Gwen's curiosity in everything Lakeland. For nearly two decades, Frances and Suzie were her constant companions, and over that time she generated an archive of almost 1000 images of the local countryside and its people. She followed the changing seasons of the farming year, capturing the moods of a nation at war and peace.

Her photographs perfectly portray the different feel of the Lake District during wartime. In order to maintain food supplies, the War Agricultural Executive Committee had been set up. Out of this, local committees were formed which had powers to direct farm holdings to plough up land, in proportion to the size of the farm, to grow crops. Regardless of whether the land was suitable for arable farming, the order had to be accepted and much pasture land went under the plough for the first time.

There are many images of farmers tending crops beside lakes and under mountains where today sheep graze. Some crops were good, but others were a complete failure. Yet wartime did provide advantages for farming. No longer did farmers have to wonder how they would sell their produce as, suddenly, there was a market for everything, with the Ministry of Agriculture buying at a fixed price. Against this changing social backdrop, Gwen's photographs give a fresh insight into this unique period of Lakeland's past.

Gwen was never renowned as a photographer in her day, although as a keen enthusiast, she often sent photographs and sometime articles to magazines. Occasionally, she had success, and her work was printed in *The Field* magazine. However, more often than not a polite rejection note was all she received. The picture of Crummock Water on page 97 of this book was among a number she submitted to *Home Words* magazine only to receive this rebuttal from its editor: 'Crummock Water is the best of these, but even this needs a darker base: otherwise it is overweighted by the tree. In the others, composition is the fault.' Today's reader may consider the validity of such a judgement. Given such lack of recognition, it is even more remarkable that she should have captured a time, a place and its people with such intimate humanity.

It was Lakeland which provided her with a unique inspiration, and when Frances died in the early 1950s, Gwen lost more than a friend: her zeal for photography went too. She left the Lake District and never went back. On her own death, her photographic archive extended little outside the Lake District, save for a few photographs of the Alps and family portraits. It was as if she never picked up a camera again.

With Frances' death and her departure from Brockstones, Gwen retreated once again into the restless solitude of her childhood. She left not only the Lake District, but England.

Gwen Bertelsman (centre with glasses) at Baddesley Clinton Roman Catholic Primary School in 1990. By this time she was known as Jane-Francis. It was the head teacher at the school, Ann Crossley, sitting to her right, who donated Gwen's photographs to the Friends of the Lake District.

In 1957, she was appointed by Dublin Universities Mission as a hospital manager in the Anglican Diocese of Chota Nagpur in India, where she remained for nearly twenty-five years. When she finally returned to England in the 1980s, it must have seemed like a foreign land. Despite her fierce independence, her pampered upbringing meant she had never learnt how to look after herself, and the life she had chosen meant she had never needed to learn.

She was not a good cook or a competent housekeeper. Perhaps this is why she sought close friendships with others. Once back in England, with nowhere to call her own, she clung to the Anglican Church, attaching herself to various monasteries. During this time she met Sister Francesa. She soon adopted the role of Gwen's mentor, as Frances Lewis had been. Sister Francesa converted to Roman Catholicism, joining the Poor Clares at their convent at Baddesley Clinton in Warwickshire. A few weeks later Gwen joined her as a guest at the convent. Here she became known as Jane-Francis; even her name was no longer her own.

Here she rekindled her love of cars, buying a Morris 1000 Traveller in which she used to make trips into nearby Chadwick End, where she worked at a nursery garden. At the end of a simple life, her pleasures remained simple: home, gardening and friendship.

Gwen seems to have spent her life searching: English-born, but with German parents, no family and few friends close enough to really know her. She had never set down roots, never married nor owned her own home. All she kept with her was her faith. But even that was not constant: a Christian Scientist in her youth, employed by an Anglican missionary organisation in middle age and living in a Catholic convent in her last days.

Gwen was a keen walker, spending much time in the mountains, as illustrated in this photograph. Frances Lewis, dressed in the outdoor equipment of the time, is last across the stepping stones.

After her death in 1994, at her request her ashes were scattered in the woods behind Brockstones; the one place where she had been truly content seemed the most appropriate for her final resting place. There can be no doubt that her days spent with her car and camera in Lakeland were the happiest of her life.

Gwen left few possessions at the end of her life of wandering. But amongst them was a battered box of disorganised photographs and negatives that was donated to the Friends of the Lake District and from which the images in this book have been taken. These photographs are an honest portrayal of Lakeland people living Lakeland lives. They speak of the seasons, of the backbreaking work of life on the land, of how families and communities worked and played together, shaping the Lakeland landscape with a cultural richness which has now disappeared. But they also reveal something more. Not only does Gwen Bertelsman's collection tell us a story about the Lake District, it is also our only insight into the private world of the woman herself.

Martin Varley

The Friends of the Lake District

The Friends of the Lake District works to keep the distinctive qualities of the landscape of the Lake District and Cumbria special. We are a registered charity with nearly 7000 members. We were formed in 1934 and over the last seven decades have been involved in a range of issues relating to the Lake District, including the campaign for its designation as a National Park.

Gwen Bertelsman joined the Friends of the Lake District in 1947 and in 1963 became a life member for the princely sum of £10.10.0. Those concerned with keeping the Lake District and the rest of Cumbria as a place as special as it was for Gwen Bertelsman can become members for an equally reasonable fee today.

For more information please contact:

Friends of the Lake District, Freepost LA1186, Kendal, Cumbria LA9 8BR. Tel: 01539 720788

Or visit our website at www.fld.org.uk

Acknowledgements

This book has been the work of a team of dedicated researchers who have a love of the Lake District and an interest in exploring its cultural heritage. They have spent many hours investigating the photographs. Many local people have also shown a keen interest in the book and have been a considerable help in telling the stories behind the pictures. Without their assistance this book would have remained a pile of dusty negatives in a box. We thank the following people for their help: Mr P. Allonby, Mrs D. Armstrong, Mr and Mrs T.A. Atkinson, Craig and Bunty Beaty, Bill Bewley, David Birkett, Johnny Birkett, Mr Brass, Victor Brownlee, Joan Clarke, Ann and Rod Crossley, Maureen Fleming, Mr J. Freeman, Thomas Gibson, R.J. Geldard, Vic Gregg, Jean Harding, Peggy Harrison, Martha Hart, Mr J Howe, Robert and Martha Jackson, John Jackson, Ted and Sheila Jenkinson, Alan Lord, Ronny Mitchell, Des and Margaret Oliver, Mr. C. Ottway, Mr and Mrs Parsons, Mike Patty, Hubert and Mabel Pilkington, Sylvia Pilling, Mr D. Sowerby, Frank and Jean Strong, Mrs D Taylforth, Mr R Taylforth, Ruth Tyson, Catherine Wakeling, John and Caroline Watson, Joan Whitworth, Mrs M. Whitwell, Mr R. Wightman, David and Janet Woodhead and any others who have helped in the production of this book.

The Photographs

Kendal to Staveley

Even in the 1940s, scything was often used for cutting awkward corners or irregular surfaces not easily mown by machine. It was a difficult art to master, but in competent hands about an acre a day could be cut.

The long pole scythe was typical of the Kendal area; the longer shaft was said to give better balance. At the top of the shaft, a sharpening stone can be seen.

The scythe was superseded by the horse-drawn mower. This was usually right-handed with a four-foot cutter bar, operated by a crank geared to the wheels. Horse-drawn mowers could mow about an acre an hour. In many cases the whole family was involved in harvesting and here, the Jordan family are using a horse-drawn mower to harvest cereals at Oaks Farm, Ambleside. It was a two-man, or in this case a man and boy, operation; the first driving and the second controlling the fall of the crop from a seat over the wheel. When sufficient for a sheaf had been cut, the rack was lowered by releasing a foot pedal and the loose corn was swept off the rack with a triangular 'putting-off' rake. The sheaf was gathered together and hand-tied with a handful of straw passed round the sheaf, twisted tight and tucked under to hold it in place. In this photograph, two men can be seen in the distance tying sheaves.

Much of the land in this picture has now been built on.

Better-off farmers replaced the horse-drawn mower with the 'self-binder'. This picture shows a self-binder working at Toadpool Farm, Kendal. John Gibson is driving the tractor while his brother Thomas operates the self-binder. The cut corn fell onto a moving canvas belt which carried it up to the 'knotter'. This bound the sheaves with twine and threw them aside with maybe 20 or 30 sheaves down the length of a field in rows or 'cuts'.

The Gibson family farm at Toadpool Farm to this day.

Stooks at Toadpool Farm, Kendal. After they had been gathered, the stooks were left to stand, allowing the wind to blow through and dry the sheaves.

This view has changed much since the 1940s, the bottom left-hand corner of this field is now part of the Plumgarths roundabout and the Kendal bypass now bisects the field to the right.

'Stooking' sheaves at Toadpool Farm, Kendal. Once the sheaves were cut they were gathered up or 'stooked' into groups, typically containing six or eight sheaves, known as 'hattocks' or 'stooks'. This photograph shows men stooking, each man collecting two sheaves to prop against the first pair standing in the centre of the photo.

'Stooking' sheaves at Toadpool Farm, Kendal. Most practices were still heavily labour-intensive and harvesting was no exception. As well as the men stooking, you can see the self-binder working on the brow of the hill.

Kendal Golf Course now occupies the ridge on the horizon.

George Geldard and Wilson Atkinson loading sheaves at Plumgarths Farm, Kendal. Once the sheaves were dry, they were collected and stacked ready for threshing.

The Geldard family farmed at Plumgarths, but now farm at Low Foulshaw and run Plumgarths as a farm shop.

Later the sheaves were removed from the stack and threshed to release the corn. This was often done by gangs who moved from farm to farm during the winter. The threshing equipment comprised a traction engine, a threshing machine and an accommodation unit. Threshers had an itinerant existence, living a rough-and-ready life on the road. The process slowly disappeared with the advent of the combine harvester.

The Leeming children bottle feeding a lamb at High Plumgarths Farm.

The Leemings farmed at High Plumgarths until 1944, when Wilson Atkinson took over. His son Tony and Tony's wife Janet farmed there after him until 2003.

Norman Armstrong of Sandy Hill Farm, Staveley ploughing oat stubble with a swing plough. The horse's collar with the high peak is more typical of Scotland and the Borders. It was considered more decorative and was used by Norman for show purposes. With show days cancelled during wartime, the collar was put to more practical use.

The Dales Way footpath now follows the far side of the wall in the middle distance. The gateway has since been built up, but the trees on the skyline can still be seen and are now over 100 years old.

Nancy Price feeding turkeys at Sunny Brow Farm, Staveley. Nancy Price was a famous actress in her time. She began her stage career in 1899, playing nearly 450 roles and produced almost 90 plays. In 1933 she became the Honorary Director of the People's National Theatre. She was also a prolific writer, the author of 21 books, several of them about the landscape, traditions and people of Westmorland. She was awarded the CBE, and died in 1970. Although she lived in Worthing, she had a fond attachment to the Lake District and often stayed at Ings with her friend Miss Martindale.

Nancy Price and Mrs Robinson. Mrs Robinson lived in the first of the four almshouses at Grassgarth, Ings. The almshouses, each with its own garden, were built in 1743 under the terms of the will of Robert Bateman, a local boy who became a wealthy merchant in Leghorn, Italy.

Mrs Robinson in her almshouse garden. Her husband worked at Ings Mill, then a bobbin mill and now a caravan site. She was very involved in the local community and sang in the choir at Ings church. She probably became a tenant of the almshouse when she was widowed.

Joseph Swift, itinerant labourer. During the war there was a great flow in and out of the Lake District of such workers who responded to the shortfall in labour as a result of conscription. Joseph Swift worked on farms around Crook.

An itinerant scissors-and-knife sharpener in Kendal. The foot pedal turned the large wheel to drive the grindstone. The machine could be tipped forwards so that the wheel could be used as a road wheel between stops. Some versions were adaptations of bicycles and could be ridden when not in use.

Windermere to Coniston

The Wightman family loading hay at Grove Farm, below Bannerigg, Windermere. Father is on the cart while his two daughters lead the horse. Correct loading of each forkful of hay was essential for stability of the load and ease of unloading into the barn at the end of the day. A long-handled 'reaching' fork, as is being used here, was essential.

The Wightmans left Grove Farm in 1947, but still live in the area.

Sheaves at Satterthwaite.

Loading hay at Colthouse, Hawkshead, using the long-handled 'reaching' fork.
Hawkshead church and the Coniston Fells can be seen in the distance.

Loading hay at Colthouse, Hawkshead.

Knotts Farm

Jack Harrison and his son Jack, riding Bessie and her daughter Fanny, at Knotts Farm, on the A592 near Holehird. Jack the elder also had three daughters, Mary, Joan and Dorothy. Knotts Farm is now a house and holiday cottages and would be unrecognisable to the Harrisons today. Young Jack is now retired.

His nephew, Alan, farms with his wife at Longmire Farm close to Knotts Farm.

The two Jacks feeding Large White piglets at Knotts Farm. The piglets are the progeny of the farm's boar Roger, by all accounts a promiscuous pig well-known to sows all over the county.

Jack Harrison supervising Jack the younger shearing a sheep at Knotts Farm.

Jack Harrison feeding poultry at Knotts Farm, Windermere. The lake is visible behind the trees.

Jack Harrison and daughter Mary (now Mrs Whitwell) with a lively calf at Knotts Farm. Mary still lives nearby.

Dorothy Harrison feeding ducks at Knotts Farm, with the houses of Troutbeck in the distance.

Ploughing a field north of Low Wood Hotel, Ambleside with a swing plough. In the 1940s there were two common types of plough, the swing plough and the wheeled plough. The swing plough was a very basic design which relied on the skill of the ploughman to maintain an even depth. It is clear from this photograph that the ploughman was struggling to keep the plough under control.

Ploughing with a wheeled plough above the A591 at Waterhead, Ambleside. The wheeled plough was a later development. The two wheels were set at different heights, one running in the bottom of the furrow and the other on the unploughed land at the side. These wheels can be clearly seen in the picture. The wheeled plough was easier to manage, but with either there was always the risk of the plough hitting a stone and the handles rising up, with considerable risk of injury.

This scene has changed irrevocably over the last sixty years. The steep land being ploughed now has houses on it. In the middle distance is Ambleside Park and immediately in front of it are the timeshare complex and houses on Maciver Lane. Part of the field above the ploughman's head now contains the Waterhead car park and houses occupy the right-hand edge of the photograph.

Lancelot Constable ploughing with a wheeled plough below the track from
Waterhead to Skelghyll Wood, Ambleside.

A tandem operation at Staveley-in-Cartmel. Here the men are ploughing with
a third type of plough, the ridging plough, while sowing at the same time.

Road watchman, near Ambleside. The brazier, a basket mounted on a metal chassis, kept him warm, and wheels and handles allowed it to be moved easily. The Stop/Go sign had a paraffin lamp on top for night-time use. Employing a night-watchman was a frequent practice on roadworks.

Children playing under Bridge House, Ambleside. Bridge House is one of the best-known buildings in the Lake District. It was originally a garden house for nearby Ambleside Hall, but was bought by the National Trust in 1928 when it was threatened with demolition.

Rushbearing

Rushbearing at Ambleside. The rushbearing ceremony is an ancient tradition stretching back to times when churches had earth floors. Sweet-smelling rushes were strewn within the church to purify the air and help insulate worshippers from the cold. The practice gradually declined during the 1800s, as church floors were flagged. The custom still continues in five Cumbrian churches, including St Mary's in Ambleside, where the rushbearing takes place on the first Sunday in July.

During the rushbearing ceremony, rushes and wild flowers were paraded round the village in procession. It ended with rushes being strewn on the floor of St Mary's Church.

The ceremony involved a cross made of rushes or flowers being carried by the children of the parish.

Traditionally the children of Grasmere and Ambleside were given a piece of Grasmere gingerbread if they carried rushes.

The jetty at Waterhead, Ambleside. The jetty looks a quiet place. There would have been few visitors during wartime. The holiday season began later in the year and there were also travel restrictions with fuel rationing.

Low Millerground, Windermere, on the shore of the lake. This was the site of an earlier ferry across the lake. A bell, which once hung in the arch over the end of the house, was used to call the ferryman and is now in the Windermere Steamboat Museum.

Turning hay at Calgarth, Windermere.

In 1940, a huge hangar and slipway was constructed here for the Sunderland flying-boat factory. The boathouse in the distance has now gone and little remains of the jetty.

Mary Millray photographed at Troutbeck in 1953. Mary was a keen needlewoman. Her husband worked for Fells Engineering of Troutbeck Bridge, which manufactured woodworking machinery.

Mary Millray feeding chickens at Troutbeck. The house in the photograph was rendered just prior to the disastrous floods of June 1953, which washed out many local roads.

Skating at Storrs, Windermere, Winter 1942. There were several hard winters in the 1940s. Eighteen inches of snow fell in some parts of the Lake District in 1940, and the road over Birker Moor was blocked until March. The winters of 1941 and 1942 were similarly bad. But the hard winters did have an advantage as the lakes froze over, turning them into an icy playground for children and adults alike.

Skating on Windermere.

Snowploughs at Troutbeck Bridge. The headlight on the snowplough shows that this is a wartime photograph. During wartime, blackout regulations required lights on all vehicles to be masked. When lights were dipped, only the nearside lamp operated and shone on the kerb, so only one lamp needed to be masked. The white-painted front was to improve visibility for oncoming vehicles.

Swarthmoor Hall on the outskirts of Ulverston. The hall was built in 1586 and has a long association with George Fox and the Quaker movement. It was a building of great interest to Gwen Bertelsman, and formed the subject of the following letter to an unspecified magazine. One of the photographs reproduced here is probably that referred to in the letter (opposite).

'Sir – I enclose a photograph of Swarthmoor Hall, Ulverston, which, apart from its fame as the residence of George Fox and an early centre of a religious movement, is of great interest architecturally. It was built at the beginning of the seventeenth century by one George Fell, a prosperous attorney-at-law, and was restored between 1913 and 1919 by a descendant of the family.

'Its walls are of grey freestone, which in the course of time have been plastered or pebble-dashed. It has stone-mullioned windows and one fine bay window which goes up through three storeys. The roof of local slate makes the house harmonize perfectly with the fells around it.

'The oak staircase is a remarkable feature of the house, and there is only one other like it in the country. It consists of a hollow square of four oak posts going from the bottom to the top of the house, round which runs the staircase in groups of four treads and little landings.

'The rooms are high and beautifully proportioned, and well lit from east, south and west. The house was originally panelled throughout, but now only two bedrooms retain the original panelling and carving. One is entered through an unusual porch or waiting room, with carved panels round the top. The original handmade and ornamented latch is still there. All round the room, at the top of the panelling, is carving, showing the lozenge which was part of the Fell coat of arms.

'The fireplace has some fine carving, deep and bold in design, which resembles that in the choir of Cartmel Priory Church, and which was probably done by the same Belgian or German craftsman. It has been described as "some of the finest made since the Reformation". In the south-east corner of the room is a second doorway leading to a little lobby, which has on one side a clothes cupboard, on the door of which is a "cock's head hinge", and opposite is a doorway opening on to a balcony from which George Fox preached to those gathered in the garden.

'At the top of the house are high lofts, with oak beams in as good condition as when they were put in three hundred years ago. The second bedroom with the original panelling has a beautifully shaped bay window, looking over the little brook in the garden across fields and woods to Morecambe Bay, and to Ingleborough and the Yorkshire fells thirty miles distant.'

It is not known whether the letter or photograph were ever published.

Cars parked above Tarn Hows.

Hawkshead Courthouse, in use in the 1950s as a National Trust forestry depot for the Hawkshead forester, Anthony Barnes. The Courthouse is all that remains of a medieval manorial farm, which once belonged to Furness Abbey. After passing through numerous hands it was given to the Trust in 1932.

Boon Crag Farm, Coniston. The farm stretches to the north shores of Coniston Water, and was the home farm for the Monk Coniston estate. It was bought by the National Trust in 1945.

Earthing-up potatoes with a ridging plough, near Coniston. This encouraged the plant to produce more potatoes. It was a tricky job because of the difficulty of managing a plough in a growing crop. Ploughing is sometimes referred to locally as 'stitching', an old English word which simply means to form a ridge and furrow with a plough. This procedure would have been known as 'stitching up potatoes'.

Yew Tree Farm Coniston, with its famous spinning gallery. The farm was once owned by Beatrix Potter and was bought by the National Trust in 1930. The Atkinson family were the tenants at the time of Gwen Bertelsman's visit. It is still run as a farm and guesthouse.

Mrs Atkinson and son Michael outside Yew Tree Farm.

Jean Atkinson outside Yew Tree Farm.

Jean Atkinson beneath Yew Tree Farm's spinning gallery.

Ruth's Story

Ruth Birkett was born in 1933 at Side House Farm, Great Langdale. She was one of seven children, having five brothers, one her twin, and an older sister. When she was six, the family moved to High Yewdale Farm, including her uncle, Ezekiel Myers, who lived with them. It was during this time, probably in the early 1940s, that Gwen Bertelsman visited the farm.

The farming communities were close-knit and hardworking, constantly helping each other out. All the family had jobs. Ruth's main task at the weekend was to prepare the kindling. Because she was a girl, Ruth's other duties tended to be household ones like cooking, cleaning and preparing the oil lamps, but she also helped with milking, lambing, haymaking and feeding the dogs and puppies. 'Jobs came first and then we could play,' recalls Ruth.

There was a range of animals on the farm including cows, sheep, hens, turkeys and geese as well as three or four horses. During the war, like other Lakeland farms, they had to plough land that had previously never taken a crop. They grew oats, potatoes, carrots, cabbages, mangolds, kale and turnips in a three-year rotation. Apart from groceries like tea and sugar, they were almost self-sufficient. They baked their own bread and sometimes churned their own butter when there was a surplus of milk.

School was in Coniston, and the children considered themselves lucky because they were taken each morning by pony and trap when Ruth's father went to drop off the milk. At night they walked back.

Until 1942, when she handed the farm over to the National Trust, Beatrix Potter was the landlady at High Yewdale and was a frequent visitor. 'I would stand back and speak to her with respect,' said Ruth. 'I knew Beatrix wrote books, and reading them, I recognised nooks and crannies described in the stories as being based on High Yewdale Farm.' Some of the field names at High Yewdale are ones used in *The Fairy Caravan*.

There was no thought of any other life. They did not want to venture far anyway during the war, because they could hear bombs dropping in Barrow. During the war, they would sometimes take in evacuees from London, usually mothers with children. They occupied one bedroom and one sitting room, where they did their own cooking by paraffin stove. After the war, the farm began to offer bed and breakfast. 'Mother took visitors for dinner, bed and breakfast so there was always plenty to do,' Ruth remembers.

Ruth worked at home until she married in 1955, when she moved to Broad Rayne Farm in Grasmere. Her husband died in 1992. To no one's surprise, in 1996, Ruth, a person with farming in her blood, moved in with her son at Moor Farm, Keswick, where she still lives.

Ruth and twin brother Johnny on the railings outside High Yewdale Farm. Johnny Birkett took over the tenancy at High Yewdale Farm from his father Bob.

Ruth and Jean Atkinson, from neighbouring Yew Tree Farm, preparing kindling wood at High Yewdale. The girls are wearing wool jumpers, wool skirts, three-quarter wool socks and always wore clogs, even to school.

Ruth's uncle, Ezekiel Myers, and her brother George outside High Yewdale Farm, Coniston. Later George took over the tenancy of Birk How Farm, Little Langdale. The farmhouse was given to the National Trust by Beatrix Potter.

Grasmere and Rydal

Drying hay was crucial. Here Anthony Chapman of Nab Farm (now Nab Cottage), on the shore of Rydal Water, and his son are out late one summer's evening making hay into 'cocks', in case there was a heavy dew or shower overnight. The field is within sight of Gwen Bertelsman's home at Brockstones.

Cyclists take a breather ascending Dunmail Raise.

Rydal Water.

The end of the day – descending from Grisedale Tarn towards Grasmere

Fisherman at Rydal Water.

Skating on Rydal Water.

Skating on Rydal Water in front of Nab Cottage.

The girls of Huyton Hill School, Liverpool, were evacuated to the Lake District during the war. The younger girls were housed at Blackwell Hall, now an arts centre, and the older girls were housed at Rydal. The photograph, taken at Rydal Water in 1942, shows most of the girls in school uniform. However, regulations were relaxed due to clothes rationing.

Tobogganing on the track from Brockstones to White Moss car park.

Rowe's van at Town End, Grasmere. Benny and Raymond Rowe had grocery shops in Windermere and Coniston. Here groceries are being delivered on the road down from White Moss, close to Dove Cottage.

A wintry scene in Grasmere, taken from the churchyard near the Gingerbread Shop. The land behind the group of men is now a garden centre. Conditions were severe enough for chains to have been attached to the rear wheels of the vehicle.

Nab Cottage on the shores of Rydal Water was once the home of Hartley Coleridge. Hartley was a shy and melancholy man, who struggled to establish his literary reputation in the shadow of his more famous father, the Lakeland poet Samuel Taylor Coleridge. He moved to Nab Cottage in 1837, and died there twelve years later. It is now an English Language Centre.

Gwen Bertelsman's picture of Dove Cottage at Rydal shows that its appearance has changed little since the 1940s. Even the walled garden and iron railings on the right of the picture remain the same. William and Dorothy Wordsworth lived here from 1799 to 1808.

Gwen's companion Frances Lewis picking bluebells on Loughrigg Fell.

Gathering sheep on the lane leading to Brockstones. When she was living at Brockstones, coming across a local farmer moving his sheep would have been a common sight for Gwen.

Shepherding above Dunmail Raise, Helm Crag rising behind.

A shepherd at White Moss Tarn.

Langdale

Haymaking at Middlefell Farm, Langdale.

Haymaking near Dungeon Ghyll, Langdale.

Gathering sheep in Langdale.

Looking towards Stool End Farm and the Band.

Gathering sheep in Langdale.

A shepherd with sheepdog, looking towards Scafell, with an eye out for stragglers.

Gathering sheep at Three Tarns, between Crinkle Crags and Bow Fell.

Vic's Story

Vic Gregg was born in 1920. When he was twelve, his family moved to Eskdale where his father, Joe, took over the tenancy of Taw House Farm, a National Trust property. They lived there for four years, before moving to Millbeck Farm, Great Langdale. It was while at Millbeck Farm that Vic and his father were photographed by Gwen Bertelsman.

The move to Millbeck was brought about by Beatrix Potter. Joe had previously sold her the stock for her farm at Near Sawrey, and she came to Taw House one day in her chauffeur-driven car to ask him to find a 'tup' for her Herdwicks. 'She wanted the best and instructed Joe to pay whatever was necessary,' recalls Vic. He went to Keswick and bought one for her. She appreciated the Greggs' help to the end of her life.

Her husband was the National Trust agent at Ambleside. When she heard through him that the tenancy of Millbeck Farm was becoming available, she told Vic's father straight away. 'Early the next morning,' said Vic, 'Joe walked over Hardknott and Wrynose Passes to Elterwater, from where he took the bus to Kendal to see the bank manager. Afterwards he went to Ambleside to arrange the tenancy, then walked back to Eskdale. He was wearing his Herdwick jacket and though it rained all day, he kept bone dry.'

Vic now lives at Chapel Stile, Langdale.

Taw House Farm, Eskdale where Vic Gregg lived 1932–36. This National Trust property has changed little since Gwen Bertelsman took this picture.

Vic moving sheep above Millbeck Farm.

Vic cutting kale for cattle feed.

Vic loading a cart with kale. During wartime in Langdale, as in other parts of the Lake District, land which had never been ploughed in living memory was put under the plough. A three-year cycle of cultivation was common: oats in the first year, kale, turnips and potatoes in the second, and oats underpinned with grass in the third. In Langdale the soil was poor and ploughs often hit stones, when the handles would fly upwards. On one occasion, Vic recalls being knocked unconscious by the handles of a plough after it hit a stone.

Vic's father Joe, with a load of cut kale. The farm's name is just about visible on the side of the cart.

Felling timber at Blea Tarn. The Scots pines between the road and Blea Tarn Woods were being clear-felled. They are thought to have been planted around 1850 to provide a picturesque foreground for long views to the Langdale Pikes.

The road from Blea Tarn into Great Langdale looking up Mickleden to Rossett Gill, at a time when walkers made up most of the traffic.

Looking towards the Scafell Range from Bowfell.

Old Dungeon Ghyll Hotel, Langdale. This former farmhouse became a popular venue for rock climbers in the Langdale Valley, and is still a popular resting place for walkers. It was given to the National Trust in 1929.

Eskdale and the Duddon Valley

A horse-drawn mower in action at Penny Hill Farm, Eskdale.

Cockley Beck Farm. This is one of the most remote farms in Lakeland, located at the junction of the Dunnerdale road and the Wrynose–Hardknott Pass road. It was given to the National Trust in 1929.

Dale Head Farm in the Duddon Valley. The farm was bought by the National Trust in 1929. Gwen Bertelsman's visit coincided with the period when the tenants were also operating a Youth Hostel. It is now leased to Leeds University as a climbing hut. The land is farmed by Cockley Beck Farm.

With no pesticides, weeds were a persistent problem. Here, at Taw House Farm, beneath Hardknott Pass, the farm worker uses a grubber to loosen weeds. In the background others are weeding with hoes.

Scafell Pinnacle.

Arthur Irving shearing sheep in Eskdale.

Arthur Irving was a well-known figure in Eskdale and later became the huntsman with the Eskdale and Ennerdale Foxhounds. He was renowned as a maker of shepherd's sticks, using ram's horns for the handle. Sheep were vital to farming in the Lake District. Not only did they provide an income for farmers, but they also were their staple food.

Robert Jackson, who farmed for many years in Eskdale, including throughout the war years, describes how important they were.

'And then every few weeks through winter, father would go and kill a Herdwick. A sheep lasted us about three weeks. Sometimes mother used to salt the hind-quarters. It was really excellent eating. I don't know whether it was hunger or what it was, but I know in the big snow of 1940 it froze afterwards and my elder brother and me went up on to the fell. We were diggin' sheep out behind the fell wall all day and we came back and I don't think I tasted anything as good to eat. They say hunger is the best sauce and I think that was it!'

Arthur Irving clearing weeds with a 'scarifier' at Penny Hill Farm Eskdale, under the shadow of Harter Fell. The scarifier comprised a number of hoe blades on a light frame capable of being adjusted to different widths to suit the spacing of the rows. It was often referred to locally as a 'stitch harrow'.

Buttermere and Crummock Water

Thinning turnips at Buttermere. Turnips provided excellent feed for cattle and were a staple produce of most farms. Many a farmer of the time has a tale to tell of working on hands and knees trying to separate weeds from turnip seedlings. One problem arising from farming previously unploughed land was the dormant weed seed which, thankful for the light and air, always flourished far better than the planted crop. It was a laborious and thankless occupation – at 18 inches (.45m) between each row a one acre field would hold 5½ miles (8.85km) of turnips.

Raking loose hay from the side of a load prior to roping up and travelling to the farm at Buttermere. The use of a mechanical elevator allowed for a higher load with less work.

Ploughing at Buttermere.

Skimming stones on Buttermere.

Buttermere and Haystacks.

View from the summit of Fleetwith Pike, looking over Buttermere and Crummock Water.

A peaceful scene at Crummock Water.

Around Keswick

Frank, John and Tom Bainbridge weeding and thinning turnips at Stonethwaite
in 1944.

A horse-drawn mower in use near Rosthwaite in Borrowdale, showing the horses' harness.

The mower had two levers which are clearly seen in this picture. The short lever set the height of the cutter bar and the long lever allowed it to be raised clear of the crop for manoeuvring.

Mowing a swathe of hay at Stonethwaite, Borrowdale. Grass dries better standing than lying, so mowing was usually done in the morning after the dew had evaporated.

The mower is coming to the end of the swathe and preparing to turn. With no pesticides meadows had many more flowers than today.

The farmer can be seen here clearing the end of the swathe, which has to be done before he can continue to cut the bottom side.

Bernard Kitching, identifiable by his distinctive headwear, raking hay at Barrow
Point on the east side of Derwent Water. The land is now part of the National-
Trust-owned Ashness Farm on the road to Watendlath.

Bernard Kitching raking hay beside Derwent Water. The rolled hay has been gathered up into a small stack or 'pike'.

Looking north towards Skiddaw.

Bernard Kitching harvesting corn by Derwent Water, looking south towards Rosthwaite.

Ashness Bridge.

The packhorse bridge at Watendlath.

John Tyson driving Old Dandy through Watendlath. John was one of two brothers who married two sisters and both families spent their lives farming in Watendlath. John was wounded in the First World War and lost a thumb, which is maybe why he is holding the reins in his left hand and hiding the other hand. He is smoking a briar pipe shaped like a bull's head. When he was sixty-six, he died from a violent dose of flu and the pipe was said to have been placed with him in his coffin.

At one time 12 to 14 families lived in the hamlet, which has buildings dating back to the twelfth century. The barn seen on the left of the picture is now demolished, but the square stones are still there, evidence that there was once a building where the wall now stands. The white house, Caffle House, is now a café run by John's great-nephew, Peter Tyson. The barn in the foreground is still standing.

Competitors in a hedge-laying competition in Borrowdale.

Bowderstone cottage, Borrowdale. A visit to the Bowder Stone, in woodlands near Grange, has been a popular excursion since tourists first visited the Lake District. Bowderstone Cottage was built in 1789 as a summer home for Joseph Pocklington of Derwent Island. Later inhabitants sold refreshments, and teas were still being advertised on the day of Gwen Bertelsman's visit. There is also a rack of postcards outside the door. It is now owned by the National Trust.

Derwent Water and Skiddaw.

Scything a damp meadow at High Lodore Farm, Borrowdale. The land here is often under water and may have been too wet for machinery.

On the path up Cat Bells from Manesty.

Ted's Story

Ted Jenkinson was born at Hollows Farm in 1935. He was the youngest of five children and lived there until he was married in 1957. As well as being a working farm, Hollows was also one of the first Youth Hostels in Cumbria, as it would have been when Gwen Bertelsman visited. It had originally been an old coaching inn, catching the passing travellers from the time when the road came down Borrowdale from Honister Pass and behind Castle Crag to Grange.

Ted's father kept mainly sheep because most of the land was on the fellside, but some cattle were kept along with hens, turkeys, geese and ducks. During the war, the War Agriculture Committee told them to use all the land so oats, corn, cabbages, turnips, cauliflowers and potatoes were also grown. In an early example of farm diversification, Ted's mother ran the hostel, sometimes taking up to 30 guests who could be walkers or cyclists, often in one large party. Many a time, scouts camping further along the river would come for their meals too, so there would have to be two sittings. The charges were as follows: bed 1s.6d. (7½p); breakfast 1s.6d. (7½p); dinner 1s.6d. (7½p); packed lunch 9d. (3¾p), and 6d. (2½p) to hire a sleeping bag. Sixpence (2½p) per person per night had to be handed over to the YHA.

There were four dormitories each sleeping eight people and one smaller one sleeping four. Meals in the dining room were waitress service or the guest could opt for self-catering, which took place in the family kitchen on a Cumberland range. Heat rose from here so the dormitories were warm. The farmhouse was lit by candles and Tilley lamps. All the children were expected to help, both on the farm and in the hostel. Ted had to bring the cows down for milking from Grange after he got off the school bus. Homework could never be started before 7 or 8pm because of all the jobs which had to be done. 'Such a regime meant I grew up fast,' said Ted. 'At fifteen, I was running the hostel single-handed while my mother had to spend time in hospital.'

The hostel was open all the year round, even on Christmas Day. But the busiest time was in the summer, when the farm children had to sleep in a wooden hut behind the farmhouse. The hostel closed in the late 1960s, but Hollows Farm remains a busy working farm to this day. Ted now lives at High Hill, Keswick.

Hollows Farm, Grange, Borrowdale.

The Bland family shearing at Nook Farm, Rosthwaite. The farm was bought by the National Trust in 1946.

Stockley Bridge, Seathwaite. This view is almost identical today.

Checking the route on Esk Hause.

Seathwaite Farm, Borrowdale dates back to 1663. Since the 1930s, the farm has been one of the most popular starting points for walks into the high fells at the heart of the Lake District. This photograph was taken in the late 1930s, yet the buildings have changed little, apart from the cottages having been whitewashed. The chimneys, walls, gateways and sheep-pen are still there, though the only trees to survive are the white lilac on the first corner and the now very tall ash, visible behind the third chimney. The rather well-dressed man and little girl were probably visitors looking for accommodation, as was the cyclist. Years of visitors' books are still kept at the end farmhouse, and all three cottages once did full afternoon teas.

Originally, the track continued to Rain Gauge Cottage – whose name reflects its fame as the wettest inhabited place in England (3 metres a year) – and on to High House Farm. Not surprisingly, flooding was a constant problem, with water frequently lapping in and out of the houses until 1966, when remedial action on the river bank solved the problem.

The farm had no telephone until the late fifties, and electricity did not come until 1962. Even then the hamlet was often was cut off in bad winters with snow reaching to the top of the pen walls with sheep escaping over it. But, as long as they had a store of paraffin and yeast, they could survive.

The block carts seen in the photograph were used well into the 1950s. A bicycle is leant against a wooden frame, known as 'shelving' or 'flakes'. This sat on top of the cart so that a wider load could be carried. It was used for harvesting bracken, an important crop for bedding.

Seathwaite Farm's oldest resident is Stan Edmondson. Born in the middle cottage in 1924, he has lived there all his life. It is now owned by the National Trust.

Show time at the Keswick Ram Fair. The annual Ram Fair was a big day in the farmers' year. Even during wartime, farmers donned their best and headed into town. The fair was held at High Hill Farm Keswick, then owned by Hal Raven. Attached to the auctioneer's box are the show conditions, which had to be displayed. Sheep were sold out of the back of a cattle trailer, such as that seen in the background operated by Frank Coates of Distington.

Billy Wilson with his champion Herdwick ram. Billy was a noted breeder. His trouser bottoms are kept out of the mud with strings known as 'yorks'.

Evacuees working on farmland near Keswick.

Picking daisies near Keswick.

John Robinson of Little Crosthwaithe Farm taking a load of hay along the A591 Keswick-Carlisle road, with Causey Pike in the distance. The horses are pulling simple 'block' carts with wooden wheels and metal rims. Little Crosthwaite Farm is now run by the Calvert Trust.

Improvisation is an essential ingredient on any farm. Here at Little Crosthwaite Farm, an inverted sledge is being used as a leveller to flatten land after sowing. The hill in the distance is Lord's Seat.

Everyone in the family was involved in farming. Here a small boy is riding a horse pulling a chain harrow on land near Keswick. A chain harrow was used to break up any lumps in grassland and make it easier to mow at haytime.

Mid-morning and a well-deserved tea break, also known as 'baggin time'. Father and son are enjoying a brew. The horses were pulling a wheeled plough near Keswick.

Picking potatoes at Goosewell Farm, near Keswick.

Bassenthwaite Lake and Skiddaw, from what is now the Whinlatter Forest Park.

On the road to Matterdale.

A busy day at Kirkhouse Farm, Dunthwaite near Cockermouth. This photograph shows the farm early in the morning. The milk churns have just been brought to the milk stand and the farmer is chatting with Frances Lewis.

Ploughing and fertilising a potato field at Kirkhouse Farm. A pair of horses pull a ridging plough, while the farmer's sons spread heaps of manure along the furrows. Out in front, the farmer spreads fertiliser from a bucket. Fertiliser was known locally as 'till' or 'bag muck'.

Thirlmere

Farming potatoes at Thirlspot Farm. Here manure is being carted to the field
prior to spreading.

Spreading manure in the furrows prior to sowing. The furrows are ridged to suit
the gauge of the block cart.

Sowing potatoes at Thirlspot Farm. Helvellyn can be seen in the background.

Harrowing at Bram Cragg Farm, St John's in the Vale. Like much farm activity, this involved traversing up and down the field on foot behind the horses. Here a spiked harrow is being used to break down the ridges on ploughed land at sowing time.

Nicolas Stephenson of Bram Crag Farm cradles a lamb on the A591 near Castle Rock, St John's in the Vale. Nicolas was one of two men who farmed at Bram Crag. It was very much a family business; he even married his partner's sister.

Ernie Brownrigg shepherding for the Manchester Water Corporation above Thirlmere. Ernie lived at West Head Farm, Wythburn, and is buried at Wythburn church. He is the only shepherd ever to have received an MBE for services to sheep.

Marking lambs at Thirlmere.

Frank's Story

Frank Strong was born in 1928. When he was eleven, he moved with his aunt and uncle to Lowthwaite Farm, St John's in the Vale. In spring 1942, on one of her customary rides, Gwen Bertelsman drove up to the farm in her Austin 7 car, a rare sight during wartime, and asked if she could take some pictures. 'I had never seen her before, and was feeding lambs at the time, so that's the picture she took," said Frank. "She also asked me to pose with one of the pigs kept on the farm. I never saw her again, but she did send me copies of the photographs, just as she had promised she would.'

Wartime was difficult, but Frank enjoyed it at Lowthwaite. 'The family could not afford to hire men, so it was needs must and everyone got on with it,' he recalls. 'My jobs were mainly with the animals, feeding, cleaning out and collecting eggs, which I really enjoyed.'

On a typical day he would have to feed the animals and sometimes help with the milking before school, which was a 2-mile walk away. He was home at 4pm then would have tea and work until supper, a substantial meal at about 7 or 8pm. Then it was out to work again until dark, which in summer could sometimes be until midnight.

He was well-fed as, during the war, the farm kept hens, ducks, geese, pigs, sheep, cattle and a goat. Potatoes and turnips were grown and so were oats to make porridge. Kale was also grown. There were plenty of logs for fires, but there was also an abundance of draughts. 'In winter, I can remember lying in bed with snowflakes drifting down on my head.'

There was no question of boredom. The only time he wasn't working was Sunday afternoon, when he'd play with other children from neighbouring farms, either walking or going for bike rides. The farming community was closely knit, helping one another and passing on news by word of mouth as few people had telephones. Such camaraderie was good for farms.

Frank left school at fourteen, but the farm could not support both him and his cousin, so he was sent to work on a farm at Ennerdale. Frank recalls: 'his was like being at the back of beyond with nothing to do and nowhere to go in my spare time.' So after six months, he came back to Keswick and worked on farms in the area. At twenty-two, he stopped working on the farms, but always worked outdoors up to his retirement. He now lives in Keswick.

Frank feeding young lambs from a sauce bottle. He is wearing clothes typical of the day: clogs, riding breeches and a V-necked woollen pullover with an open-necked flannel shirt and a wool jacket.

Frank with a pig, one of 56 kept on the farm.

Frank feeding young lambs, with the mother looking on. A goat was kept to provide early milk until the mother's milk came. Also in the background is Tewitt Tarn surrounded by a wood, long since disappeared. The trees were felled during the war to make pit props.

Sosgill Bridge, Vale of St John's, with Blencathra in the distance. The two children
are thought to be Bunty and John Jackson.

Fornside Farm, St John's in the Vale, with Sosgill Bridge in the distance. The land was farmed by John Jackson and here one of his sons is bringing the cows home for milking. John Jackson is now in his nineties and lives in the Newlands Valley.

Eric Harding with his pet fox, Tarzan, at Threlkeld in 1942. Eric was born in 1921. His father worked at Threlkeld Quarry, but in 1944, Eric joined the Border Regiment, based at Carlisle. Two years later he married Jean. After leaving the Army he became a Forester. He died in 1992, aged seventy. Jean Harding still lives in the Thirlmere Valley.

Bill and Martha's Story

The Nag's Head inn was closed in 1929 and converted into two cottages. John Bewley and his wife moved into one of the cottages in 1935 with their children Bill and Martha and an older son. His wife had worked at the inn prior to its conversion and John worked for Manchester Corporation, which owned the whole valley apart from Wythburn church. Eric and Jean Harding (see page 137) lived in the other cottage during their early married life, from 1948–50.

The sloping tin roof in the photograph covered the kitchen and the room above was the bathroom, which had a freestanding zinc bath, that had to be emptied manually. 'We could get straight down to the lake shore from the back door,' remembers Bill, 'but we weren't allowed to swim or paddle because of fear of pollution.' This was also the reason why burials were stopped in Wythburn churchyard.

During wartime, Wythburn school, which was situated in what is now the church car park, was temporarily closed. Martha had to stay with relatives at Legburthwaite in order to attend the school there, in what became Thirlmere Youth Hostel.

'For about two and a half years I had walked to Legburnthwaite on Sunday nights and back home after school on Fridays,', Martha recalls.

Bill left the school at fourteen and went to work for Manchester Corporation where subsequently he became reservoir manager for Thirlmere, a position he held for the rest of his career.

Martha had joined the Woman's Royal Navy Service, married a sailor and moved away to Folkstone, where she lived for fifty-one years. Later, when both her husband and Bill's wife had died, she returned to her Thirlmere roots. She now lives with her brother in the valley where he was born, educated, worked and has spent all his life.

The cottages were demolished in the early 1950s amid fears about sewage seeping into the lake.

The old Nags Head Inn, Wythburn. The inn was situated across the road from the present day Wythburn church. It was frequented by the Wordsworths, Hartley Coleridge and Christopher North among others, and John Keats stayed there in 1818. In Baddeley's *Guide to the Lake District*, it was described as a 'snug little hostelry'.

The Nags Head Inn cottages, Wythburn.

Woodworking at Steel End. Forestry has long been a major industry in the Lake District, particularly around Thirlmere. Steel End, at the southern end of the lake, had a large timber yard.

Man and horse dragging or 'snigging' timber, west of Steel End.

West End Farm, Steel End. The shed at the far left has gone, but the rest of the buildings still remain. Traces of the banking can still be seen but the rest has reverted to pasture. The men operating the saw are also in the photograph opposite.

Ullswater

Harvesting potatoes at Hartsop Hall, Patterdale. Farming was a 'reserved' occupation during the war, as it was essential for the nation's food supply. In a time when labour was in short supply, gangs of contract labourers would often work their way across the county.

Hay 'shaker' or 'tedder' at Side Farm, Patterdale, looking north towards Glencoyne Park.

On Helvellyn looking north-east towards Ullswater.